THE WOR
DICKENS

MICHAEL ST JOHN PARKER

The England of Charles Dickens' birth was Regency England, still locked in a life and-death struggle with the French Emperor Napoleon; it was aristocratic in its politics, agricultural in its economy, and racy in its morals. During Dickens' lifetime, the nation was taken to an unprecedented peak of power and prosperity by commerce, industry and the vigour of a fervently respectable middle class. At the same time, there were undercurrents of insecurity and anxiety, both social and private, together with economic instability, and well-founded fears of violence.

Dickens' novels bear the stamp of the turbulent period in which his life was lived. They convey a strong sense of rejection of the past: progress and reform are all the vogue. On the other hand, Dickens shared with many of his contemporaries an anxious alarm about the heartless destructiveness of the many forces unleashed by the Industrial Revolution. Thus all his work is shot through with contradictions: the champion of the middle classes was also their severest critic, the passionate advocate of reform was fearful of revolution, the idealist was also an often despairing realist and materialist.

RIGHT: Gustave Doré's engraving conveys the crowded, hectic, sometimes nightmarish quality of life in mid-Victorian London.

A KENTISH CHILDHOOD

Charles Dickens' family background was socially modest – his grandparents on his father's side had been domestic servants. His father, John, was a clerk in the Navy Pay Office, earning a salary of less than £200 a year when Charles was born – a sociable, charming man whose utter fecklessness with money brought increasing misery to his whole family.

Charles' mother, Elizabeth, has been represented in the character of Mrs Nickleby as snobbish and socially pushing, domineering but domestically inept, demanding but ultimately somewhat casual in her relations with her children, rather hard and rather silly. On the other hand, it is at least possible that Charles was driven by feelings of rejection to portray his mother unfairly. The family nurse, Mary Weller, described her as 'a dear, good mother and a fine woman', and one of Dickens' earliest and most knowledgeable biographers reports him as saying that 'his first desire for knowledge and his earliest passion for reading were awakened by his mother'. Elizabeth's ineffectual attempts to achieve a genteel status for her family may have earned her son's contempt, but she was perhaps more influential than he was willing to admit in setting the targets of his own life's work.

ABOVE: The house in Portsea, Portsmouth, then known as 1, Mile End Terrace, Landport, where Charles Dickens was born in 1812. It is now a museum devoted to his memory.

BACKGROUND PICTURE: This view of Chatham Dockyard in the early 19th century closely resembles what the young Charles Dickens would have seen from his childhood home at 2, Ordnance Terrace across the hayfield with 'the two beautiful hawthorn-trees, the hedge, the turf, and all those buttercups and daisies . . .'.

The happiest phase of Charles' childhood was between 1817 and 1822, when his father held a good post in the Chatham Dockyard and the family lived at 2, Ordnance Terrace, Chatham. The house faced, at that time, a big hayfield which was covered in summertime with buttercups and daisies, while in the distance was the winding River Medway, with the sailing ships gliding up and down. There he spent the impressionable years from five to ten, playing in the house or its surrounds, visiting the Dockyard, the Gun Wharf and the Rope Walk with his father, sometimes even cruising to Sheerness; his father took him on expeditions to explore the drowsy old cathedral city of Rochester, with its crumbling castle circled by cawing rooks, or to the woods and parkland round the great house at Cobham. It was an enchanted time, and in later years when the strain of work became too heavy, or the ideas would not flow, or personal problems threatened, he would escape to Kent; and, if he could not go in person, he would send his characters.

Above: The interior of one of the rooms at the Dickens Birthplace Museum. Mrs Dickens would probably have been delighted by the appearance of modest elegance seen here – in reality, daily life in the Dickens household was a crowded affair.

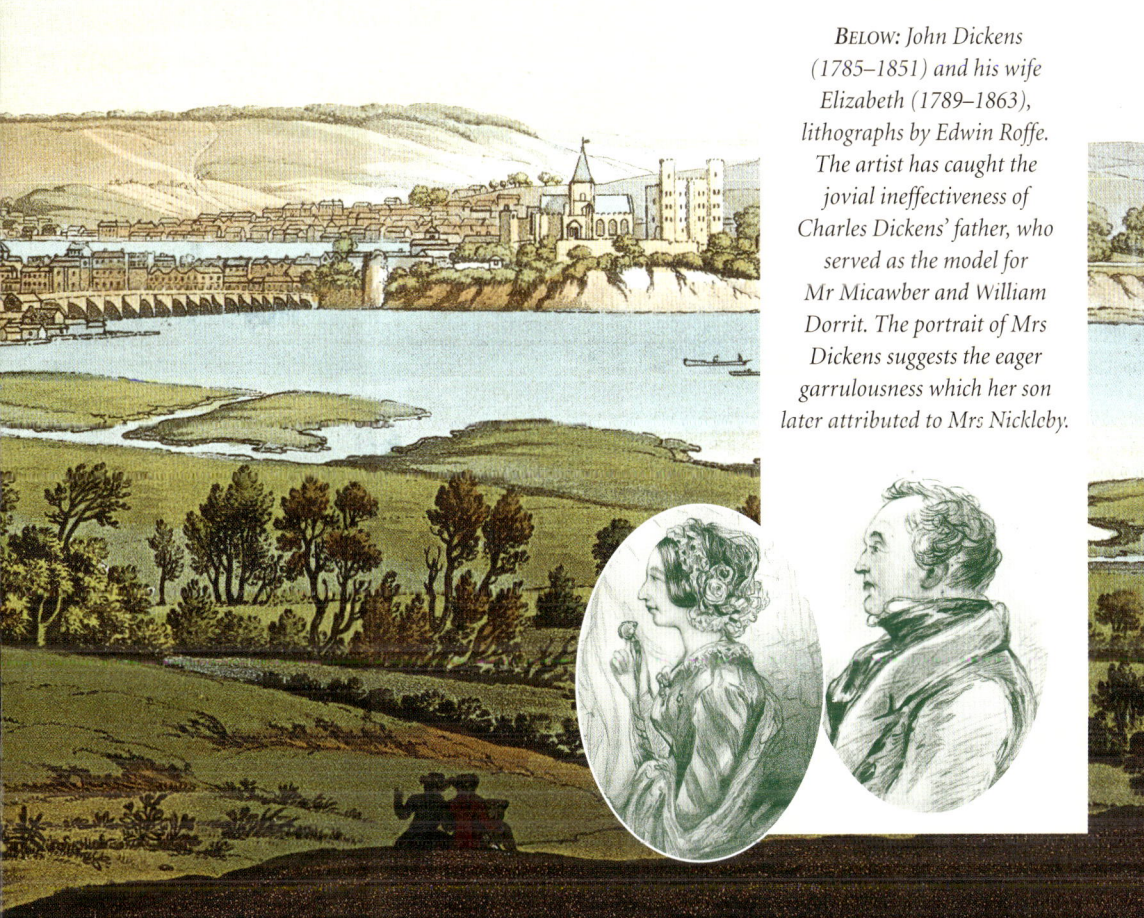

Below: John Dickens (1785–1851) and his wife Elizabeth (1789–1863), lithographs by Edwin Roffe. The artist has caught the jovial ineffectiveness of Charles Dickens' father, who served as the model for Mr Micawber and William Dorrit. The portrait of Mrs Dickens suggests the eager garrulousness which her son later attributed to Mrs Nickleby.

THE EARLY YEARS

'Speaking of memory one day, he said ... it was a mistake to fancy children ever forgot anything.' Dickens' happy early recollections of Kent were to be quickly overlaid by a very different set of impressions after his family moved in 1822 to London. Crowded into a two-up, two-down terraced cottage – there was also a basement and a tiny garret – were the Dickens parents, their five children, a servant, and a lodger named James Lamert, a relative by marriage.

However, the overwhelming impressions of squalor which marked Dickens' later recollections of this period were chiefly born of his father's unmanageable slide into catastrophic debt.

Charles' schooling was discontinued, and after a while he was called upon to contribute to the family funds. James Lamert found him a job sealing and labelling pots of blacking in a warehouse off the Strand, but the conditions were sordid and even the slight indulgence allowed to him, of working on his own at the front of the premises, carried with it the further degradation of labouring in the public view.

Meanwhile, his father's troubles came to a climax with his imprisonment in the Marshalsea Debtors' Prison. The family was temporarily broken up, and Charles had to live alone in lodgings. When, after about six months, John Dickens was released, he decided to take him away from the warehouse, but Charles's mother wanted him to continue, saying that the family could not afford to lose the money he was earning. The boy could never forgive her this hardness.

Beyond doubt, the months in Warren's warehouse and the time of his father's imprisonment scarred Dickens for life.

ABOVE: 16, Bayham Street, Camden Town, in London, saw the beginning of young Charles Dickens' childhood miseries. He was distressed immediately on his arrival there to find that there were no plans for him to continue his schooling.

RIGHT: Early 19th-century engraving of a child giving alms to a debtor imprisoned in the Marshalsea Prison. Dickens' childhood memories of the miseries inflicted on his family during John Dickens' imprisonment for debt inspired him in due course to write Little Dorrit.

Throughout his books he details the horrors of child-exploitation, the fate of orphans and abandoned children, and the effects of improvidence and debt. He rarely spoke directly about his own experience of these things, though he tried to relieve it by writing a fragment of candid autobiography. However, he could not go through with it and took refuge in fiction, reliving his own past through the character of David Copperfield.

ABOVE AND LEFT: Warren's shoe-blacking warehouse was situated beside Hungerford Stairs, which ran down to the River Thames from the Strand. Dickens could never forget the scuffling sound of the rats which infested the rotten old building in which he had to pass so many unhappy hours.

OPPOSITE: The cover of one of the original monthly instalments of Little Dorrit. *The centrepiece shows the heroine emerging from the gateway of Marshalsea Prison.*

LEFT: The slums of London in the mid-19th century were places of desperate poverty and squalor. Dickens' portrayal, in Oliver Twist, *of the human rat-packs which populated these places did much to mobilize public opinion in favour of schemes for social improvement.*

JOURNALIST AND RACONTEUR

Right: This is the earliest known portrait of Charles Dickens, painted when he was 18, by his aunt. Here is the dashing young reporter, keen to cut a figure and rise above the miseries of his childhood.

Below: War and Peace *and* Pickwick Papers *have been nominated as the world's two greatest novels. Dickens' first great fictional creation has never lost its place in the public's affection. Here Mr Pickwick addresses the circle of his admiring friends.*

John Dickens used to say of his famous son in later life that he 'may be said to have educated himself!' This may have been a little less than fair to Wellington House Academy in the Hampstead Road, where Charles was a pupil for more than three years, from 1824 to 1827.

At the age of fifteen, however, his mother took him away and set him to 'a proper career' in a solicitor's office: an unsuccessful experiment which gave Dickens a marked and enduring dislike of the law and lawyers.

In a manner typical of his age, though, he was resolved to better himself, and set about learning the Gurney method of shorthand writing. Thus armed, he branched out as a freelance law reporter, and then, during 1830–33, as a parliamentary reporter. This was a period of tumultuous activity in parliament, when the debates over constitutional reform, which ultimately issued in the Great Reform Bill of 1832, spilt over into public demonstrations and rioting, and looked at times as if they might provide the spark for revolution. Neither side commended itself to

Dickens, who found the reactionaries contemptible and the radicals alarming.

During 1833–35 he travelled the country, covering a wide range of happenings. 'I have often transcribed for the printer from my shorthand notes, important public speeches in which the strictest accuracy was required, and a mistake in which would have been to a young man severely compromising, writing on the palm of my hand, by the light of a dark lantern, in a postchaise and four, galloping through a wild country, all through the dead of night, at the then surprising rate of fifteen miles an hour.'

The assorted observations and experiences of these early years were incorporated in Dickens' first published works *Collected Sketches by Boz* (1836) and *Pickwick Papers* (1836–37). *The Sketches* are drawn by a sharp-eyed, precociously perceptive, often cruelly funny reporter; their success depends as much on the author's powers of observation as on his talents of expression. *Pickwick*, on the other hand, sees the emergence, unevenly perhaps, but decisively, of a creative genius and one of the great masters of English prose.

ABOVE: *A page of Dickens' shorthand script. The Gurney system was supposed to take three years to learn. He mastered it in three months.*

ABOVE LEFT: *A fanciful depiction of Dickens as, 'with fear and trembling', he delivers his first manuscript for publication in 1833.*

LEFT: *The Houses of Parliament were burnt down on the night of 16 October 1834. The fire, which started accidentally, came to be widely seen as a symbol of the destruction of an antiquated system of government; it did not, however, purge Dickens' own disillusionment with the political process.*

THE LONDONER

BACKGROUND PICTURE: London's river furnished settings for some of Dickens' most dramatic passages in his novels. This study captures both the grim practicality of the river's commercial activity, and also its brooding mystery.

BELOW RIGHT: Charles Dickens depicted in a stained-glass panel, on display in the dining room of Dickens House Museum.

Dickens is conspicuously, indeed for many people supremely, the novelist of London. But the London that he loved, and described with such enthralling vividness and power, was the London of his youth and early manhood, of which the picture, accumulated in countless details, through innumerable hours of wanderings, was indelibly etched upon the retina of his imagination. And this, as Dickens' biographer Peter Ackroyd has observed, 'was a city with its heart still in the eighteenth century' – a city smaller, more chaotic, more picturesque, more violent, more squalid, more richly varied than its Victorian successor. 'The major thoroughfares were already lit by the new gas, but this was not the bright and even glow of the late Victorian period: the light flared and diminished, casting a flickering light across the streets and lending to the houses and pedestrians a faintly unreal, or even theatrical quality.'

All through his life, Dickens drew strength and inspiration from immersing himself in the turbid stream of London life. Writing from Switzerland in 1846, shortly after beginning work on *Dombey and Son*, he lamented his exile from the busy streets: 'It seems as if they supply something to my brain, which it cannot bear, when busy, to lose ... A day in London sets me up again and starts me. But the toil and labour of writing, day after day, without that magic lantern is immense!'

From the days of his earliest childhood, he was accustomed to travelling long distances on foot, whether to work – a round trip of ten miles from his lodgings in Hampstead to Warren's blacking warehouse and back again – or simply as a rambler. And not withstanding the innumerable and notorious dangers of the capital, he was an inveterate night-walker, pacing from dusk to dawn in order to work off the inner tumult of his mind and tirelessly collect fresh material. He spoke with his own voice in *Barnaby Rudge*: 'To pace the echoing stones from hour to hour, counting the dull chimes of the clocks; to watch the lights twinkling in chamber windows, to think what happy forgetfulness each house shuts in ...'.

ABOVE: Odd relics of an older London, which had survived the building developments of the 18th century, and perhaps even the Great Fire of 1667, still survived here and there to catch Dickens' imagination and delight his sense of the picturesque. This old house, on the corner of Portsmouth Street, served as the model for The Old Curiosity Shop. *It can still be seen today.*

LEFT: Covent Garden Market at 4 o'clock in the morning. In youth and middle age, Dickens liked nothing better than to explore the streets of London by night and day, observing its crowded and turbulent life. Covent Garden, where the consignments of fruit and flowers from the country arrived, was a particularly vibrant centre of excitements and contrasts.

LIVING IN THE PAST

Dickens seems to have approached the writing of his first historical novel, *Barnaby Rudge*, about the Gordon Riots of 1780, partly in the spirit of a challenge to Sir Walter Scott. But the inspiration which directly spurred him on to write came in the shape of the Chartist movement which developed from 1838 onwards, and seemed at times to threaten the fabric of English society. 'Dickens feared lawlessness but understood the motives of those who rose up against authority . . . just as his own troubled relationship with his father lends further depth to his presentation of a world in which most forms of lawful authority are corrupt or corrupting' (Peter Ackroyd).

Barnaby Rudge, the fantastic, harmless simpleton, and Grip, his very knowing raven. The bird was inspired directly by Dickens' family pet of the same name; the boy in the novel stands for simplicity in human nature.

A Tale of Two Cities (1859) was even more carefully researched than *Barnaby Rudge*. Dickens had been much struck by Carlyle's masterly *History of the French Revolution* which had appeared twenty-two years earlier and was able, as one great man to another, to draw directly on Carlyle's help, which was given in the form of a 'cartload' of books, all of which Dickens read, or at least looked at. But once again the immediate motive for writing was direct and contemporary, though this time it was tied up with Dickens' own personal situation and pre-occupations: the themes were imprisonment, the need for self-sacrifice, and the renunciation of love – all of them intensely pertinent to the unhappy state of Dickens' own life at that time. The literary critic Angus Wilson has expressed the view that with these themes Dickens enters the world of the great nineteenth-century Russian novelists Tolstoy and Dostoevsky. Nor is it just the choice of these that sets *A Tale of Two Cities* apart from the rest of Dickens' work – the approach is also distinctive, shorn of several of the elements which are usually central: dialogue, sub-plot and melodrama.

STORMING OF THE BASTILLE
A contemporary lithograph of the taking of the Bastille, 14 July 1789. The horrors of the French Revolution were burnt deep into the minds of Englishmen in the early 19th century, and Dickens shared the common fear of uncontrollable social disorder.

LEFT: *Dickens' view of Temple Bar – he called it a 'leaden-headed old obstruction' – suggests something of his attitude towards the past. He was not interested in it for its own sake, nor did he see it as preferable to his own time. He would draw lessons from it if he could, and otherwise he would discard it.*

LEFT: *Contemporary print of the 'Burning, Plundering and Destruction of Newgate Prison' on 7 June 1780, an episode in the Gordon Riots which figured in Barnaby Rudge. Dickens was both fascinated and horrified by such outbreaks of anarchy.*

THE FAMILY MAN

'The Victorians wanted Dickens' novels as nobody these days really wants anybody's novels. They were the great family entertainment, with something for everybody – an exciting story for Papa, fun for the boys, sentiment for Mama and the girls.' The essential background to Dickens' success, as J. B. Priestley defines it here, was the Victorian achievement of family life.

During the first three-quarters of the nineteenth century, advances in medical science, technology and economics in England made it possible as never before for people to live in extended family groups, often three generations together, with uncles, aunts, cousins and relatives by marriage tacked on. These clusters were not created out of mere sociability; the death rate remained high, and many people, young and old, would have been left on their own if they had not been able to appeal to more fortunate relatives for support – which could now be given more readily than ever before, thanks to the growing prosperity of the Victorian era.

Reality, as ever, was closely followed by ideal – the importance of the family was magnified, family relationships were codified – in short, 'family values' were invented by the early Victorians.

Charles Dickens played a central part in this hugely important process. The theme of the family, whether

Above: 48, Doughty Street, Mecklenburgh Square, Dickens' home from 1837 to 1839, saw both brilliant success and personal unhappiness for the young author; it was here that Dickens wrote Pickwick Papers, Oliver Twist *and* Nicholas Nickleby, *and here that his sister-in-law Mary Hogarth died.*

Inset Above:
Four of Dickens' children – Charley, Mamie, Katey and Wally – sketched by Maclise. The family's pet raven, Grip, perches on the back of the sofa.

triumphant or distressed, was central to all his novels, and the more he wrote of it, the more he was read. His chosen method of publication, by monthly or weekly instalments, was peculiarly well-adapted to intensify the 'family' element of his work by encouraging the practice of family reading, which grew enormously in popularity among the middle classes as a way of spending the evening.

The fact that Dickens' own family, at all age levels, would be described by a modern sociologist as seriously dysfunctional does not invalidate the quality of Dickens' contributions to the family ideal. His preoccupations with incompetent parenthood, child abuse, the consequences of financial irresponsibility, the perils of love and the pains of death, achieve all the more poignancy as reflections of Dickens' own trials and tribulations.

ABOVE: Bob Cratchit carries the crippled Tiny Tim home to Christmas dinner. Modern critics are inclined to condemn A Christmas Carol *as sentimental, but Tiny Tim's plight touched the hearts of Dickens' contemporaries.*

LEFT: Mr Fezziwig's Ball, from A Christmas Carol. *Dickens popularized the concept of Christmas as a festival of family reunion.*

FAR LEFT: A particularly harrowing episode *of* Dombey and Son *is read in the family circle after dinner. Instalments of Dickens' novels were awaited with passionate excitement.*

DICKENS' WOMEN

ABOVE: Maria Beadnell, the object of Dickens' first serious love affair and perhaps the cause of his lifelong unhappiness with women, portrayed here in costume as a milkmaid.

RIGHT: Mary, second of the three Hogarth sisters. Her sudden death at the age of 18 inspired some of Dickens' most powerful sentimental writing, notably Little Nell's deathbed scene in The Old Curiosity Shop.

It serves no useful purpose to judge Dickens' relationships with women by twenty-first century standards. He was, in general terms, both attracted and attractive to women – often powerfully so, in both cases. Knowledgeable and uncensorious about the behaviour of others, he was rigorous and self-denying in his personal morality, and prone to sensations of guilt. His essential regard for the female sex made him all too readily disposed to place women on pedestals; at the same time, his own experiences and his sharp powers of observation made him acutely aware of the ridiculous, foolish or simply frail aspects of female behaviour, to which he responded with a mixture of mirth and exaggeration.

Dickens' personal history of relationships with the opposite sex was marked by frustrations and sadness. His first important romantic involvement came in 1829–33, when he fell in love with a girl named Maria Beadnell, a pretty, petite brunette with a lively and flirtatious manner, who kept him for a while in suspense and then dismissed him with casual thoughtlessness. He made an ill-judged marriage on the rebound, and failed to find release either in that or in the affair which was the immediate cause of the break-up of his marriage.

He married Catherine Hogarth on 2 April 1836, and spent a brief honeymoon near Chatham, before setting up house, where they were joined by Catherine's sixteen-year old sister Mary. This was a curious triangular connection; Dickens found

THE HEROINES OF DICKENS' NOVELS

For the most part, Dickens' heroines are characterized by childlike innocence, vulnerability and dependence which are far removed from the ideals of modern feminism. Sympathetically understood, however, they reveal a great deal about the complex, disappointed and guilt-ridden romanticism of their creator.
For Dickens, marriage was either ridiculous or repellent, while true love was illicit or tragic. His anti-heroines, on the other hand, such as Nancy in *Oliver Twist*, can seem stronger and more dynamic than the men who exploit them, even though social convention may require that they come to a melodramatically bad end.

little intellectual companionship in his wife – indeed, he hardly seems to have asked for it; instead, he developed an intense platonic relationship with Mary, and was completely shattered by grief when she died with startling suddenness on 7 May 1837.

In 1842, a third Hogarth sister, Georgina, joined the Dickens household and gradually became more and more important in Charles's life. So close did they become that, when Charles and his wife separated in 1858, and Georgina stayed with him, assuming the role of housekeeper in his family, rumours of an affair were not lacking.

The reality, however, was that during the course of 1857 Charles had fallen madly in love with a young actress named Ellen Ternan. There can be no doubt about the intensity of his feelings towards Ellen, with whom he spent much time in secret during the 1860s – indeed, he finally set her up in a little house in Peckham in 1867. But the precise extent of their intimacy remains unclear.

ABOVE: Ellen Ternan, the young actress whose friendship with Dickens was the occasion of the collapse of the author's marriage in 1858. She remains an enigmatic figure, whose real role in Dickens' life may never be fully understood.

INSET ABOVE: This portrait of Georgina, the third Hogarth sister, who joined the Dickens household in 1842 and stayed until the time of Charles' death in 1870, suggests something of the calm steadiness and strength of purpose which made her so much valued.

LEFT: Catherine Dickens shortly after her marriage, described as '... a pretty little woman, plump and fresh-coloured, with the large, heavy-lidded blue eyes so much admired by men.'

BREAKDOWN OF A MARRIAGE

Right: Catherine Dickens in later life. The shy glamour has been replaced by an insecure heaviness – a sad picture.

Below: Dickens rented 1, Devonshire Terrace, a large and handsome London residence, between 1839 and 1851. For much of this time, however, he was abroad.

During the early years of his marriage Dickens worked with frenzied energy, taking on more commitments than any ordinary man could have managed, and developing formidable powers as both businessman and author. There were frequent house moves and, as the years went by, extended adventures abroad. And, amid all this, there were the children – ten in all, a noisy, demanding and often, inevitably, disappointing and worrying brood.

Catherine simply could not cope, and from an early stage was affected by what evidently became endemic post-natal depression. Even for domestic purposes, household management and daily companionship, Charles turned more and more to her sisters Mary and Georgina, in turn.

It is at least possible that the picture of Catherine has been unfairly drawn. Henry Morley, one of the contributors to Dickens' own journal, *Household Words*, remarked that 'Dickens has evidently made a comfortable choice. Mrs Dickens is stout, with a round, very round, very pretty, very pleasant face, and ringlets on each side of it. One sees in five minutes that she loves her husband and her children, and has a warm heart for anybody who won't be satirical, but meet her on her own good-natured footing. We were capital friends at once, and had abundant talk together' – by no means an unattractive picture, even if a little condescendingly drawn.

Charles was less tolerant. He wrote in *Household Words* about a wife who 'is not distinguished by closeness of reasoning or presence of mind' and who on occasions 'would have gone into hysterics but that I make a rule of never permitting that disorder under my roof'. Catherine was no weakling, but she could not stand against Dickens' gigantic dynamism and, it must be said, intolerable egotism.

'Catherine and I are not made for each other,' Dickens told his friend John Forster, 'and there is no hope for us. It is not only that she makes me uneasy and unhappy, but that I make her so too – and much more so. She is exactly what you know, in the way of being amiable and complying; we are strangely ill-assorted for the bond that there is between us . . . I am often cut to the heart by thinking what a pity it is, for her own sake, that I ever fell in her way . . .'.

LEFT: *Charles Dickens with his daughters Mamie and Katey in the garden at Gad's Hill Place. They sided with him after their mother had left the family home – Mamie without reservation, though Katey later described her father as ' . . . not a good man, but he was not a fast man, but he was wonderful!'.*

BELOW: *The Dickens family outside Gad's Hill Place, purchased by Dickens just before his marriage broke up.*

STAGE-STRUCK

From his earliest childhood, Dickens was fascinated by the theatre. At the age of eight, he saw the great clown Grimaldi at the Theatre Royal in Chatham, and also first encountered Shakespeare's plays. He enjoyed building and operating his own toy theatres, sometimes employing dramatic effects such as explosions caused by firecrackers. After leaving school at the age of fifteen, he became an enthusiastic *habitué* of the London theatres. It was undoubtedly from personal observation that he wrote: 'The principal patrons at private theatres are dirty boys, low copying clerks in attorneys' offices, capacious-headed youths from city counting-houses ... all the minor theatres in London, especially the lowest, constitute the centre of a little stage-struck neighbourhood.'

His early passion for story-telling merged easily into acting. His talent for mimicry was pronounced, and he clearly had a natural talent for suggesting character, particularly through comic effects. There is clear evidence that at one time he considered a

ABOVE: Dickens bought Tavistock House, in Tavistock Square, in 1851, and fitted it out with great splendour. He also converted the large schoolroom into what he called 'The Smallest Theatre in the World', in which The Lighthouse, The Frozen Deep *and several children's plays were performed.*

RIGHT: Dickens acting in the farce Used Up, *in which he took the part of an aristocrat, Sir Charles Coldstream, whose ennui is eventually cured by the realities of simple farm life. One of his fellow actors observed of him at this time, '... he was both sensitive and irritable, and a restless disposition ... made him desirous of continually doing something'.*

theatrical career: in March 1832, the manager of the Lyceum agreed to audition him for a part in a forthcoming production, and Dickens was only prevented by a heavy cold from taking what could have been a decisive step. He seems to have given little thought to the possibility of writing for the stage, but his novels were strongly influenced by the Victorian melodrama. References to the theatre abound in Dickens' works, and in *Nicholas Nickleby* the theatrical theme is central to the plot.

During his middle years, Dickens was involved, both as manager and actor, in a series of amateur productions of increasing complexity and ambitiousness. It was while he was involved in a production of *The Frozen Deep* that he met and fell in love with Ellen Ternan.

Towards the end of his life, stage acting gave way to a different form of dramatic activity, in the shape of the series of readings from his own works, which began in 1858 and continued with ever-increasing triumph until his death.

ABOVE: *Dickens particularly enjoyed acting as Captain Bobadil in Ben Jonson's* Every Man in his Humour. *He seems to have relished the melodramatic possibilities of the cowardly, swaggering Captain, and enjoyed making up in red and black; he also wore a peaked beard and a black moustache, so that he '... looked like an old Spanish Portrait, I assure you'.*

CENTRE: *Dressing for the play, a scene from* Nicholas Nickleby. *'Here all the people were so much changed that he scarcely knew them. False hair, false colour, false calves, false muscles – they had become different beings.' Dickens was fascinated by the illusions of the theatre.*

LEFT: *It was while acting in a production of Wilkie Collins' melodrama* The Frozen Deep *in 1857 that Dickens fell in love with Ellen Ternan, one of the actresses.*

THE PUBLIC PERSONALITY

*D*ickens learnt at an early stage to live with fame – and was happy to stand in the public eye and endeavour to lead opinion. The reporter in him was never entirely dormant, and he leapt with particular enthusiasm at the opportunity given to him in 1846 to become founding editor of a great national newspaper, the *Daily News*. Here he 'flung himself into the work with a thoroughly characteristic energy'. But he could not endure the fact that ownership was in other hands than his own, and the experiment ended abruptly with his resignation.

ABOVE: As a public speaker, Dickens was happiest when working from a set text, latterly his own works. His intense, dramatic manner lent additional authority to his public appearances.

RIGHT: Dickens perches on the symbol of his brilliantly successful magazine All the Year Round. *It was this that gave him, in literary form, the public platform which he needed, and which he used to powerful effect in the later years of his life.*

In the aftermath, he thought of seeking to become a magistrate, or taking on 'some Commissionership, or Inspectorship . . . I would never rest from practically showing how important it has become to educate, on bold and comprehensive principles, the Dangerous Members of Society'. The urge to manage others for their good never left him – in 1856, at a moment of intense personal unhappiness, when he was staying on his own in Dover, he took a walk on the Downs and there met a 'tramping family in black' to whom he gave 'eighteen pence which produced great effect, with moral admonitions which produced none at all'.

By February of 1850, Dickens had founded a journal of his own, in which he could combine the roles of editor and proprietor: *Household Words*. This was to become a leading concern for the whole of the rest of his life, and a major channel of communication with his vast and ever-increasing public.

He became the prime target of all those who sought sponsorship for their good causes, or their products in advertisements; his mere appearance on a platform, as at the Leeds Mechanics' Institute in 1848, meant that 'the whole audience rose, and the applause became almost deafening'; and his son Henry later recalled that 'to walk with him in the streets of London was a revelation . . . people of all degrees and classes taking off their hats and greeting him as he passed'.

Yet there was a darker side. John Forster said of him, ' . . . the secret was that he believed himself to be entitled to higher tribute than he was always in the habit of receiving'. Perhaps a prime secret of public success is the possession of an invincible egotism.

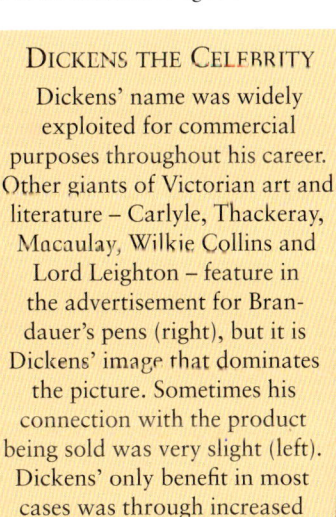

ABOVE: Dickens' foray into newspaper editorship lasted only a short time and did not distract him from what today would be seen as his novelist's vocation. To Dickens himself, however, every sort of literary effort was fascinating.

DICKENS THE CELEBRITY

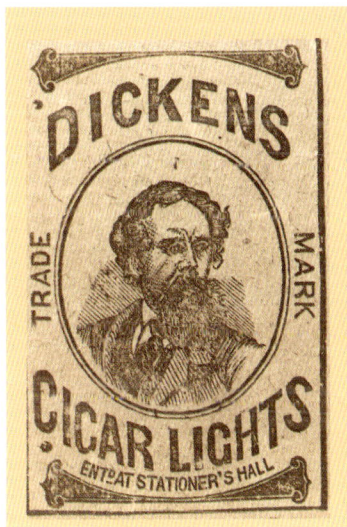

Dickens' name was widely exploited for commercial purposes throughout his career. Other giants of Victorian art and literature – Carlyle, Thackeray, Macaulay, Wilkie Collins and Lord Leighton – feature in the advertisement for Brandauer's pens (right), but it is Dickens' image that dominates the picture. Sometimes his connection with the product being sold was very slight (left). Dickens' only benefit in most cases was through increased sales of his books.

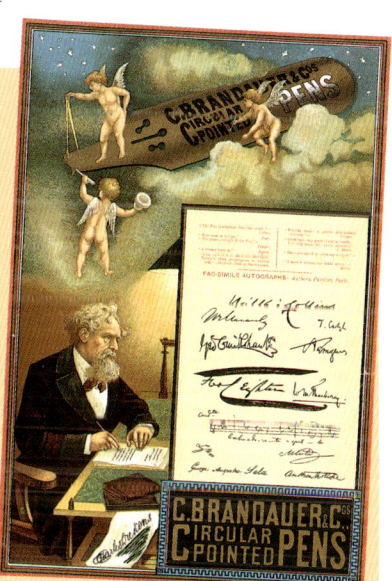

THE SOCIAL REFORMER

*I*t was a major part of Charles Dickens' achievement that he forced a reluctant, even horrified, English public to recognize the existence of abuses for which other, possibly duller, personalities were able to devise remedies. He was a publicist, and not a politician – his refusal to stand for Parliament, on more than one occasion, underlined his recognition of his own status. But that did not make him any the less a social reformer in his own way.

A random selection from the interminable list of his speeches suggests the range of his interests: the Administrative Reform Association, the Artists' Benevolent Society, the Governesses' Benevolent

ABOVE: Dickens just after the foundation of Household Words *and at the time of the publication of* Bleak House.

BACKGROUND PICTURE: These old houses in Cloth Fair, Smithfield, were slums of the very worst sort.

LEFT: 'The paths of cold-ash and huts of staring brick marked the vicinity of some great manufacturing town... Now, the clustered roofs and piles of buildings trembling with the working of engines and dimly resounding with their shrieks and throbbings; the tall chimneys vomiting forth a black vapour which hung in a dense ill-favoured cloud above the house-tops and filled the air with gloom; the clank of hammers beating upon iron, the roar of busy streets and noisy crowds...'. (The Old Curiosity Shop)

Institution, the Great Ormond Street Hospital, the Liverpool Mechanics' Institution, the Manchester Free Library, the Metropolitan Sanitary Association, the Newsvendors' Benevolent Association, the Playground and General Recreation Society, and the Royal Hospital for Incurables all received the benefit of his support.

The underlying issues emerged in his novels – the injustice and oppression of the Poor Law and the horrors of the London underworld in *Oliver Twist*, the social problem of illegitimacy and the scandal of privately run institutions for unwanted children in *Nicholas Nickleby*, the grim social consequences of the Industrial Revolution in *The Old Curiosity Shop* and *Hard Times*, the coldness of a commercial society in *Dombey and Son*, the corruption of government and the law of debt in *Little Dorrit* and the destructive degradation of the penal system in *Great Expectations* and *Our Mutual Friend*.

Finally, there were areas in which Dickens was not content to be publicist, but acted in his own right, such as the Ragged School movement, and a project to help reclaim prostitutes. In both of these he worked in close collaboration with Angela Burdett-Coutts. The plight of children, in particular, struck at the very nerve-centre of Dickens' own sensibilities: 'I have seldom seen anything so shocking as the dire neglect of soul and body exhibited in these children'. For Dickens, philanthropy was not an indulgence but a passion born of desperate need.

LEFT: '"Many thousands are in want of common necessaries: hundreds of thousands are in want of common comforts, Sir." "Are there no prisons?" asked Scrooge, "Are there no workhouses?"' Dickens' depiction of misery at Christmas time, in *A Christmas Carol*.

OPPOSITE, BELOW: Lord Shaftesbury, one of the great social reformers of the mid-19th century, visits a charity school. Dickens took a keen and constructive interest in the Ragged School movement: '... I saw 3,000 children hunted, flogged, imprisoned, but not taught ...'.

23

DICKENS AND AMERICA

RIGHT: Anti-British feeling was never far beneath the surface in 19th-century America, but Dickens' fame rose above it, to the extent that the novelist was identified with the British national symbol of the lion.

BELOW: Dickens' first visit to the USA ended sourly, largely because of his outspoken attacks on slavery. By the time of his second visit, the civil war had been fought and the slaves freed. This American cartoon of 1868 conveys the message that reconciliation was considered appropriate on both sides.

Dickens first visited the United States in 1842, to find that he had acquired a fame which staggered even his self-esteem. Excited crowds thronged around him on every possible occasion; he was fêted at a series of elaborate receptions, balls and visits; prints of him poured off the presses.

Unfortunately, not everything that he saw in America pleased Dickens. After initial delight at the warmth of his reception, he was put off by the intrusive curiosity of the multitudes; he was repelled by American table manners, by the men's habit of spitting constantly and by what he considered their general raucousness of speech and style. Finally, he was disgusted by what he saw of the institution of slavery. In short, having unreasonably expected to find a paradise on earth, he was equally extreme in his disappointment when it did not come up to scratch. He made matters even worse for himself by rebuking the Americans in a number of public speeches for their flagrant disregard of the courtesy of international copyright.

The result of all this was that he left America at the end of his first visit in a mood of sourness, which was reflected in the satire of *Martin Chuzzlewit*, published in 1843–44. As a consequence, his reputation in the United States suffered for some time to come.

Dickens did not return to America until 1868, when he was persuaded to give a series of readings which he had been developing in England since 1858. No doubt he was attracted by the idea of re-conquering a partially lost territory; more practically, there were promises of huge profits.

"A MAN AND A BROTHER."

Whatever the motivation, all expectations were exceeded: Boston, New York, Philadelphia, Baltimore, and all the cities of New England seemed to go mad for him. In New York, people stood in queues throughout freezing nights to buy tickets for his readings, and in Washington the President, Cabinet and the Supreme Court packed the audience.

The extraordinary turbulence of Dickens' relations with his American public almost defeats analysis. Perhaps a melodramatic, even desperate, strain in the author's soul found something reciprocal in the soul of the emergent nation, so that both saw something essential of themselves in the other. The final partings in New York were almost drowned in tears.

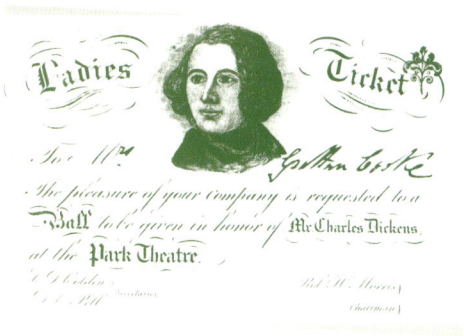

ABOVE: Dickens' first visit to America, in 1842, began amid scenes of the most extravagant enthusiasm and he was welcomed as a celebrity.

LEFT: John Bull bids farewell to Dickens, surrounded by the characters from his novels, as the author sets sail for New York city.

BELOW: A Press dinner at Delmonico's in New York, on the occasion of Charles Dickens' second visit to the USA.

25

A DREAMER OF CHARACTERS

Dickens' greatness as a novelist stands on a broad foundation, but if there is one element in his work which is above all the others, it is his power of characterization. Many of the people in his stories are in a sense 'types', but he has the knack of investing them with individuality, so that they carry complete conviction. Most were, in fact, to some extent based on real-life people, but Dickens gave them an independent vitality that was in no way dependent on their origins. They lived with him as he wrote, and he seems to have been almost possessed by them, demonstrating 'a kind of imagination, fed by the unconscious, that we do not expect to discover in a novelist', as J. B. Priestley says.

It is undeniable that some of Dickens' most memorable creations owe part of their identity in the popular mind to the inspired skill of his illustrators: sixteen artists altogether contributed to the first editions of his works, but two of them, George Cruikshank and Phiz – Hablot K. Browne – made especially distinctive and important contributions. At all times, though, Dickens remained in control of the image, and was ceaseless in giving instructions to his illustrators.

The results have, in some cases, virtually entered English folklore, as can be seen from the innumerable representations in popular art, ranging from statuettes to cigarette cards. Countless people feel they know Mr Pickwick and Mr Micawber, Fagin and Bill Sikes, Scrooge and Uriah Heep, even though they may not have read the books in which these characters appear. In this, Dickens' achievement resembles that of Shakespeare – he has contributed to the universal imagination.

Dickens and his characters: fiction became more powerful than fact in the public's perception of the author, even in his own lifetime.

ABOVE: 'Let us be moral. Let us contemplate existence.' Mr Pecksniff in Martin Chuzzlewit is one of Dickens' great creations – almost the definitive fictional hypocrite.

LEFT: Mrs Gamp, the old midwife, with her huge coal-scuttle bonnet and her umbrella, as she appears in Martin Chuzzlewit, one of Dickens' greatest comic creations.

OPPOSITE, ABOVE: '. . . in the ceaseless tumbling speech of Mrs Nickleby we catch an echo of the infant child hearing the sound of his mother's voice.' Dickens undoubtedly put many of his feelings about his mother into the character, but it is by no means intended as a simple portrait.

LEFT: Dickens' writing-desk and chair in the study at 48 Doughty Street. The desk carries the china monkey without which Dickens was unable to settle down to writing.

FULL CIRCLE

The last years of Dickens' life were a crescendo of frenzied activity, which give the unmistakable impression of a driven man trying to escape from his life's problems by unremitting, frantic work. Journalism, writing, reading tumbled over each other to the destruction of his health, though they brought him fortune and a constant enhancement of his fame. At one time, he settled in something like isolation to write at Gad's Hill Place, and tried to break with the past; in 1860 he actually made a great bonfire of all his old personal papers. But the financial strain of supporting, in effect, three separate households, following the break-up of his marriage, triggered all the neuroses born of his early insecurities, and drove him back inexorably into the public arena.

In June 1864, Dickens and Ellen Ternan had a narrow escape from death when they were involved in an appalling railway catastrophe at Staplehurst, near Folkestone. The shock of the experience inflicted severe damage on Dickens' already enfeebled constitution, and yet he went on working harder and harder with an almost suicidal energy.

Dickens' second American tour in 1868 took a further toll on his health. The punishing schedule of readings which he set for himself, involving constant travel and all the stress of a rapid sequence of appearances before over-excited crowds in stifling halls – and, still more, the immense demands which he laid on himself in his melodramatic characterizations – quite literally wrecked him.

He spent 8 June 1870 writing busily in his chalet summerhouse at Gad's Hill Place; then, at dinner that night, he had a stroke, and died the next day. On the last page that he wrote, in the unfinished *Edwin Drood*,

ABOVE: Dickens portrayed at the scene of his last reading, on 8 March 1870, when he performed Sikes and Nancy. On the way to the platform he whispered to a friend: 'I shall tear myself to pieces,' but he could not stop himself going through with it.